Basic Shapes for Beginners

A Hands-On Approach for Pre-Writing Strokes for Preschoolers

COPYRIGHT

Basic Shapes for Beginners

© 2015 Heather Greutman | GrowingHandsOnKids.com

ISBN-13: 978-1519716477 | ISBN-10: 1519716478

This publication is for personal use and educational use (one classroom or co-op group). You may make copies of the printables included in this book for your immediate family or own classroom or co-op group.

Disclaimer: I am a Certified Occupational Therapy Assistant. The advice in these tips is not a replacement for medical advice from a physician or your pediatrician. Please consult their advice if you suspect any medical or developmental issues with your child. These tips do not replace the relationship between therapist and client in a one on one treatment session with a individualized treatment plan based on their professional evaluation.

All activities are designed to be completed with adult supervision. Please use your judgment when setting up these activities for your child and do not provide items that could pose a choking hazard for young children. Never leave a child unattended when completing any of these activities. Please also be aware of all age recommendations on the products you are using with your child. The author is not liable for any injury caused to your child while completing any of these activities.

Publishing and Design Services | MelindaMartin.me

GrowingHandsOnKids.com

Basic Shapes for Beginners

A Hands-On Approach for Pre-Writing Strokes for Preschoolers

Heather Greutman

GrowingHandsOnKids.com

TABLE OF CONTENTS

HOW TO USE THIS BOOK 7
BEFORE GETTING STARTED 9

WEEK 1: VERTICAL AND HORIZONTAL LINES

Supply List 11
Day 1: Matching Vertical and Horizontal Lines 12
Day 2: Play Dough Worms 13
Day 3: Tracing Vertical and Horizontal Lines 14
Day 4: Organize Lines by Color 15
Day 5: Coloring Vertical and Horizontal Lines by Size 16
Bonus Activity: Straight Lines Sensory Bin 17

WEEK 2: CIRCLE SHAPES

Supply List 19
Day 1: Small and Big Circle Play Dough Shapes 20
Day 2: Find the Circles Scavenger Hunt 21
Day 3: Colored Pom Pom Task Tray 22
Day 4: Circle Coloring Sheet 23
Day 5: Trace or Copy Circle Shapes 24
Bonus Activity: Circle Sensory Bin 25

WEEK 3: CROSS (+) SHAPE

Supply List 27
Day 1: Crossing Midline Parade 28
Day 2: Figure 8 Motor Walk 29
Day 3: Finger Paint Copying 30
Day 4: Pipe Cleaner Matching 31
Day 5: Tracing and Copying Cross Shapes 32
Bonus Activity: Chalk Board Copying 33

GrowingHandsOnKids.com

WEEK 4: SQUARES AND RECTANGLES

- Supply List 35
- Day 1: My House is Made of Shapes Puzzle 36
- Day 2: Shaving Cream Drawing 37
- Day 3: Block Stacking and Building 38
- Day 4: Paper Strip Cutting Activity 39
- Day 5: Draw Your House 40
- Bonus Activity: Tracing and Copying Square Shapes 41

WEEK 5: X SHAPE AND DIAGONAL LINES

- Supply List 43
- Day 1: Finger Paint Brushing 44
- Day 2: Matching Diagonal and X Shape Lines 45
- Day 3: Play Dough Lines 46
- Day 4: Cotton Ball Tracing 47
- Day 5: DIY Tick Tac Toe Board 48
- Bonus Activity: Tracing and Copying Diagonal Lines / X Shape ... 49

WEEK 6: TRIANGLES AND DIAMONDS

- Supply List 51
- Day 1: Triangle and Diamond Coloring Sheet 52
- Day 2: Paper Crown Craft 53
- Day 3: Play Dough Cut Outs 54
- Day 4: Sensory Tracing 55
- Day 5: Foam Shape Stamping 56
- Bonus Activity: Q-Tip Tracing 57

RESOURCES 59
HOW TO DOWNLOAD THE PRINTABLES 60
ABOUT THE AUTHOR 61
PRINTABLES 63

GrowingHandsOnKids.com

GrowingHandsOnKids.com

HOW TO USE THIS BOOK

Before any child learns to write there are basic lines and shapes that they need to learn developmentally in order to produce legible writing. These are called pre-writing lines or strokes! Pre-writing lines consist of vertical & horizontal lines, circles, and diagonal lines to form shapes such as triangles and diamonds.

During my time working with preschool age children as an Occupational Therapy Assistant, one of the concerns I came across with children who were delayed in pre-writing skills was lack of exposure. Once children were given access to items and projects that encouraged good pre-writing lines, their handwriting skills showed a huge improvement!

That is why I have designed this hands-on unit study. I am a firm believer in kids learning through play. All of the activities are designed to provide play activities for children, exposing them to the basic pre-writing lines that are developmentally age appropriate for them!

For a quick reference, here are the common pre-writing lines and ages they are learned and mastered:

- Vertical Line - (Age 2 imitates, age 3 copies/masters)
- Horizontal Line - (Age 2 imitates, age 3 copies/masters)
- Circle - (Age 2 imitates, age 3 copies/masters)
- Cross shape (+) - (Age 3 imitates, age 4 copies)
- Right/Left Diagonal Line - (Age 4)
- Square - (Age 4)
- X shape - (Age 4)
- Triangle (Age 5)

All of the activities are designed to be completed in 6 weeks with 2 bonus shapes included at the end for children who are ahead or just for fun. However, this does not mean that you HAVE to complete these activities in 6 weeks. If you want to take your time and only do 1 or 2 activities a week instead of 1 each day, you can do that! Tailor the pace to the needs of your child.

For this age group I recommend using small broken crayons or small golf size pencils for all "writing" work. This encourages proper, age appropriate grasp on writing utensils. When children use writing utensils that are too large for their age, they have difficulty manipulating and controlling the pencil which affects their grasp and legibility.

You and your child are well on your way to developing good writing skills! Have fun and enjoy this exciting time of learning!

Blessings,

Heather Greutman

BEFORE GETTING STARTED

Using the same phrases or language when teaching pre-writing lines and strokes will help your child to develop good writing and letter formation habits later on. Here are some phrases and terms I have used when working with children.

There are different variations, but the main thing is to stick to the same phrase so that your child can associate that line with the phrase and be able to self-correct.

Vertical lines - Say "Straight line down, Start at the top, BIG line down" or "Straight line down, Start at the top, little line down." Or if size is not a concern, you can just say "Straight line down, Start at the top, down." If your child has problems with knowing when to stop, you can add "Straight line down, Start at the top, down, and STOP!"

Horizontal lines - Always model starting to left to right saying "Straight big line across", or "Straight little line across." You can also add "start at the left, straight line across, and STOP!"

Circle shape - "Start at the top, circle around, and STOP!" Circle shapes should also be made in a counterclockwise direction.

Left Diagonal Line - "Start at the top left, line sideways"

Right Diagonal Line - "Start at the top right, line sideways"

"X" - " 'X' marks the spot!"

All children under the age of 6 are in what's called a hands-on learning phase. Movement and learning in different positions is also important.

Most of these activities can be done on the tummy (tummy time), standing, kneeling, sitting "crisscross applesauce" on the floor, or at a child size table and chair. If you are using a table and chair, please make sure your child has proper body position (feet flat on the floor or a flat surface) and sitting back against their chair in an upright position. If their feet do not touch the floor, you can stack books under them, or you can get a small step stool. I like the white plastic step stools from IKEA that also have blue grippers on the bottom.

SUPPLY LIST

- Printables for week 1
- Activity/Task trays
- Small task baskets to organize with
- Plastic bin/tub
- Handwriting Without Tears Wood Piece Set for Capital Letters (Optional)
- Homemade or store bought play dough
- Small broken crayons
- Golf size or small pencils
- Colored craft pipe cleaners
- Uncooked spaghetti noodles
- Wooden craft sticks
- Wikki Stix
- Other house hold items that are straight lines (i.e. long wooden spoons, play tongs)
- Shaving cream (Optional)
- Food coloring (Optional)
- Finger paint (Optional)
- Unsharpened pencils
- Google Eyes

BASIC SHAPES FOR BEGINNERS

WEEK 1

DAY 1

VERTICAL AND HORIZONTAL LINES

ACTIVITY	AGE LEVEL	PURPOSE
Matching Horizontal & Vertical Lines	2-5 Years Old	Exposing your child to vertical and horizontal lines for writing

ITEMS NEEDED

- Printable of horizontal & vertical lines
- Craft sticks or Handwriting Without Tears Wood Piece Set for Capital Letters
- Activity Trays

DIRECTIONS

1. Print out the horizontal and vertical line printable.

2. Put it on the activity tray, placing a second smaller activity tray next to it with the wooden craft sticks or HWT Wood Pieces inside.

3. Allow your child to explore matching the sticks with the vertical or horizontal lines on the printable. Only give a demonstration of how to do this if your child asks you to. Allow them to problem solve and figure out how to do it first before stepping in.

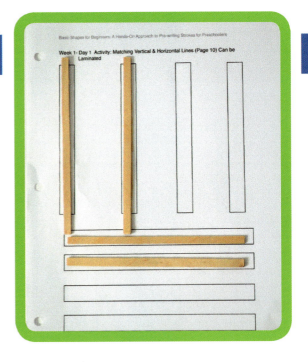

GrowingHandsOnKids.com

Basic Shapes for Beginners

Day 2

WEEK 1

VERTICAL AND HORIZONTAL LINES

ACTIVITY	AGE LEVEL	PURPOSE
Play Dough Worms	2-5 Years Old	Exposing your child to vertical and horizontal lines for writing

ITEMS NEEDED

- Homemade or store bought play dough
- Task Tray
- Google eyes

DIRECTIONS

1. Have your child roll out lines with their hands using the play dough, making play dough worms!

2. After they have made the worm like lines with their play dough, ask them to show you what straight line (vertical) or line across (horizontal) is. Give a demonstration if they ask you to. If they do not show the correct line after you ask them, you can give them a model.

3. Decorate your lines with the google eyes to make them into "worms"

GrowingHandsOnKids.com

WEEK 1

DAY 3

Basic Shapes for Beginners

VERTICAL AND HORIZONTAL LINES

ACTIVITY	AGE LEVEL	PURPOSE
Tracing Vertical & Horizontal Lines	3-5 Years Old	Exposing your child to vertical and horizontal lines for writing

ITEMS NEEDED

- Horizontal & Vertical line printable
- Small broken crayons

DIRECTIONS

1. Print out the vertical and horizontal line printable.

2. Have your child use broken crayons or a short, golf size pencil to trace the lines.

> Ages 3 and under use a sensory medium such as shaving cream, cornmeal, or finger paint and have them use their fingers to trace the lines instead of using a pencil/crayon You may laminate these pages to help the paper hold up under the sensory medium

GrowingHandsOnKids.com

Basic Shapes for Beginners

Day 4

WEEK 1

VERTICAL AND HORIZONTAL LINES

ACTIVITY	AGE LEVEL	PURPOSE
Organizing Lines by Color	2-5 Years Old	Exposing your child to vertical and horizontal lines for writing

ITEMS NEEDED

- Colored craft pipe cleaners
- Task tray
- Baskets to organize with
- Divided vegetable tray (optional)

DIRECTIONS

1. Set up one large task tray with one basket on it containing all the colored craft pipe cleaners. Have enough baskets or trays set on the sides with one pipe cleaner of each color set in it. This will help your child to know where to match the colors.

2. Have your child match the pipe cleaners to the corresponding colors in each task tray.

3. During this activity ask them to tell you what color and shape the pipe cleaners are.

Optional: Use a divided vegetable tray to have your child divide out the colored pipe cleaners in.

15

GrowingHandsOnKids.com

WEEK 1

VERTICAL AND HORIZONTAL LINES

Basic Shapes for Beginners

DAY 5

ACTIVITY	AGE LEVEL	PURPOSE
Color Vertical & Horizontal Lines by Size	2-5 Years Old	Exposing your child to vertical and horizontal lines for writing

ITEMS NEEDED

- Small, broken crayons
- Vertical & Horizontal Line Printable

DIRECTIONS

1. Print out the straight-line coloring printable. Have your child color each line with the colors stated on the printable.

2. The lines form the word "HI" in capital letters. If your child knows some of their alphabet, ask if they know what letters these lines form. If they are closer to age 5, you can also ask if they know what the letters say. This helps your child to see that straight lines down and straight lines across form letters for reading and writing.

Optional: Instead of crayons you could also use washable finger paint and brushes. Both of these activities will encourage proper hand grasp on writing utensils.

GrowingHandsOnKids.com

Basic Shapes for Beginners

BONUS ACTIVITY

WEEK 1

VERTICAL AND HORIZONTAL LINES

ACTIVITY	AGE LEVEL	PURPOSE
Straight Lines Sensory Bin	2-5 Years Old	Exposing your child to vertical and horizontal lines for writing

ITEMS NEEDED

- Plastic bin/tub
- Uncooked spaghetti noodles
- Wooden craft sticks
- Handwriting Without Tears Wood Piece Set for Capital Letters (Optional)
- Wikki Sticks
- Craft Pipe Cleaners
- Unsharpened pencils
- Other house hold items that are straight lines (i.e. long wooden spoons, play tweezers/tongs or fork)

DIRECTIONS

1. Use a bin or tub with a lid for easy storage and cleanup.

2. Mix in the various items listed above or that you find around the house.

3. Talk about each item, what shape it is, and how it can be a horizontal line or vertical line. For younger children (age 2) just allow them to explore each item mentioning colors and what each item is.

GrowingHandsOnKids.com

Basic Shapes for Beginners

GrowingHandsOnKids.com

Basic Shapes for Beginners

WEEK 2

CIRCLE SHAPES

SUPPLY LIST

- Printables for Week 2
- Activity/Task trays
- Small task baskets to organize with
- Plastic bin/tub
- Plastic divided tray (ex. plastic veggie tray)
- Medium size plastic cups (1 to 2 for pouring and dumping)
- Small, broken crayons
- Small, golf size pencil
- Small mixing spoons (such as tablespoons)
- Play dough (homemade or store bought)
- Small and Big circle cookie or play dough cutters Rolling pin (optional)
- Variety of circle shapes or items around the house (ex. balls, fruit etc).
- Variety of colored craft pom poms (sizes and colors)
- Fine Motor Tweezers or play chop sticks
- Medium size jingle bells
- Bouncing Balls
- Large plastic whiffle balls
- Shaving cream
- Food coloring
- Finger paint
- Painting bib

Basic Shapes for Beginners

WEEK 2

DAY 1

CIRCLE SHAPES

ACTIVITY	AGE LEVEL	PURPOSE
Small and Big Circle Play Dough Play	2-5 Years Old	Exposing your child to the circle shape for writing

ITEMS NEEDED

- Play Dough (Homemade or Store bought)
- Activity Tray
- Small and Big circle cookie or play dough cutters
- Rolling pin (optional)

DIRECTIONS

1. Set up the activity on a plastic or wooden task tray. If you are making the play dough yourself, have this made ahead of time.

2. Have your child flatten the play dough with their hands or a rolling pin.

3. Have your child use the circle cookie cutters (biscuit cutters work well) or play dough circle cutters to cut out small and big circle shapes in the play dough.

4. Ask them to show you which ones are big and which are small. You can also have them sort the shapes they make into small containers, one for big and one for small circle shapes.

Basic Shapes for Beginners

Day 2

WEEK 2

ACTIVITY	AGE LEVEL	PURPOSE
Find the Circles Scavenger Hunt	2-5 Years Old	To expose your child to circle shapes in their environment

ITEMS NEEDED

- Small or medium size basket or plastic bin
- Variety of circle shapes or items around the house (hidden or just placed out as usual).

DIRECTIONS

This activity can be as easy or hard as you want it to be. You can either hide certain circle items around the house and ask your child to find a certain item, or you can just go on a search around the house for anything they can see that is a circle.

You can divide it up by room, such as living room, dining room and kitchen. Or divide it up saying "find 5 things we eat that are shaped like a circle." (example would be apple, orange, grapefruit etc); "Find two things in the bathroom that are circle shapes." etc. Once you have found all the circle shape items and have placed them in the basket, take each item out and talk about what it is, what color it is, and what it's function is!

CIRCLE SHAPES

GrowingHandsOnKids.com

WEEK 2

Basic Shapes for Beginners

DAY 3

CIRCLE SHAPES

ACTIVITY	AGE LEVEL	PURPOSE
Colored Pom Pom Sorting Tray	2-5 Years Old	Exposing your child to circle shapes, colors, and sorting skills Hand strengthening for fine motor skills/pre-writing strokes

ITEMS NEEDED

- Variety of colored craft pom poms
- Plastic divided tray (ex. plastic veggie tray)
- Fine motor tweezers or play chop sticks

Ages 3 and under can use a play tablespoon to move pom poms back and forth.

DIRECTIONS

1. Place the colored pom poms into a container next to the divided tray. If you don't have a divided tray, you can just use a variety of small plastic tubs or containers set up in a row.

2. Have your child use a small fine motor tweezers or play chop sticks to pick up one small pom-pom. Remember to have your child use an age appropriate hand grasp on the tweezers or chop sticks.

3. Have them match all the pom-poms to the correct containers. For children who don't know their colors yet, simply set up a pom-pom tray like pictured below and have them practice moving pom-poms back and forth between containers.

GrowingHandsOnKids.com

Basic Shapes for Beginners

DAY 4

WEEK 2

ACTIVITY	AGE LEVEL	PURPOSE
Circle "O" Coloring Sheet	2-5 Years Old	Practice coloring skills and using proper hand grasp for pre-writing strokes

ITEMS NEEDED

- Circle "O" Coloring Sheet
- Small, broken crayons
- Small, golf size pencil

> **Ages 3 and under use a sensory medium such as shaving cream or finger paint and have them use their fingers to color instead of using a crayon**

DIRECTIONS

1. Print out the Circle "O" Coloring Sheet Printable below.

2. Have your child use crayons, colored pencils, or markers to color the coloring sheet. Remember to encourage your child to color inside the lines if age appropriate (Ages 4 1/2 to 5) and use an age appropriate hand grasp on their coloring utensils.

3. The tracing sentence is designed for ages 5+.

CIRCLE SHAPES

GrowingHandsOnKids.com

WEEK 2

Basic Shapes for Beginners

DAY 5

CIRCLE SHAPES

ACTIVITY	AGE LEVEL	PURPOSE
Trace or Copy Circle Shapes	3-5 Years Old	To practice pre-writing strokes and lines needed for letter formation

ITEMS NEEDED

- Circle shape printable
- Small, broken crayon
- Golf Size pencil

DIRECTIONS

1. Print off a copy of the circle shapes printable.

2. Have your child trace the circle shapes with a crayon or pencil using age appropriate hand grasp. Say: "Circle - start at the top, circle around, Stop!" as your child traces or copies each circle.

Ages 3 and under use a sensory medium such as shaving cream, cornmeal, or finger paint and have them use their fingers to trace the lines instead of using a pencil/crayon

3. Above age 4 should be able to stay on the writing line with minimal deviations away from it.

4. Circle shapes start at the top, and go counter clockwise to the stopping point back at the top.

GrowingHandsOnKids.com

Basic Shapes for Beginners

BONUS ACTIVITY

WEEK 2

ACTIVITY	AGE LEVEL	PURPOSE
Circle Sensory Bin	2-5 Years Old	To explore circle shapes in a variety of textures and every day items

ITEMS NEEDED

- Medium size plastic bin with a lid for easy storage
- Large & Medium size craft pom poms
- Small mixing spoons (such as tablespoons)
- Medium size Jingle Bells
- Medium size plastic cups (1 to 2 for pouring and dumping)
- Bouncing Balls
- Large plastic whiffle balls
- Any other circle shapes that you would like to add

DIRECTIONS

1. Use plastic tub or container with a lid for easy storage. Place the craft pom poms in the bottom of the bin, these are your sensory bin base.

2. Place all the circle items in the bin, on top of or partially hidden in the pom poms.

3. Allow your child to explore all the circle shapes in the bin. Please only use items that are age appropriate for your child and do not pose a choking hazard for smaller children.

CIRCLE SHAPES

GrowingHandsOnKids.com

WEEK 3

CROSS (+) SHAPE

SUPPLY LIST

- Printables for week 3
- Activity/Task trays
- Small task baskets to organize with
- Painters tape
- Music
- Chalk board or clip board
- Chalk
- Homemade or store bought finger paint
- Large pieces of painting paper
- Painting bib
- Paint brushes
- Colored craft pipe cleaners
- Small golf size pencil
- Broken crayons
- Damp wash cloth
- Shaving cream
- Food coloring
- Finger paint

Basic Shapes for Beginners

WEEK 3

DAY 1

CROSS (+) SHAPE

ACTIVITY	AGE LEVEL	PURPOSE
Crossing Midline Parade	2-5 Years Old	To promote whole body crossing midline skills, needed for drawing a cross shape

ITEMS NEEDED

- Painters tape
- Start and stop sign printable
- Music

DIRECTIONS

1. Mark off the cross shape on the floor with painters tape. Place the start sign at the top vertical line & the Stop sign on the right of the horizontal line (picture below).

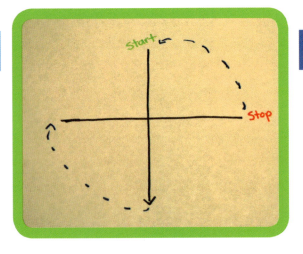

2. Have your child stand on or near the Start sign. Instruct them that once the music starts playing they are start marching following the line on the ground and touching each knee as it comes up with the opposite hand.

3. Start and stop the music as you please. When the music stops, have your child freeze in whatever position they are in when the music stopped. Then, they can unfreeze once the music starts again.

4. If your child gets lost on how to walk the cross shape, simply take small pieces of tape and connect the solid lines with the dotted pieces of tape, like below, to give them a visual of where to go next.

Basic Shapes for Beginners

Day 2

WEEK 3

ACTIVITY	AGE LEVEL	PURPOSE
Figure 8 Motor Walk	Ages 3-5	To promote whole body crossing midline skills, needed for drawing a cross shape

ITEMS NEEDED

- Painters tape laid out in a figure 8 design
- Music
- Chalk board or clip board hanging horizontally on the wall
- Chalk or small pencil/crayon

DIRECTIONS

1. Have your child walk the figure 8 pattern on the floor to the music. Have them stop and start when you turn the music on and off.

2. Once they are able to complete the figure 8 with only 1-2 cues when crossing over the middle, have them move on to the chalk board or clip board.

3. Give them the chalk, pencil or crayon and have them draw a figure 8 pattern, horizontally on the writing surface while standing. Have them continue making this pattern on the paper or chalk board 10 times.

CROSS (+) SHAPE

WEEK 3

Basic Shapes for Beginners

DAY 3

CROSS (+) SHAPE

ACTIVITY	AGE LEVEL	PURPOSE
Finger Paint Copying	2-5 Years Old	To promote practice of the cross shape (+) for pre-writing practice

ITEMS NEEDED

- Homemade or store bought finger paint
- Large pieces of paper
- Painting Bib
- Optional: Paint brushes

DIRECTIONS

1. Have your child paint cross shapes on their pieces of paper, starting with the vertical line "Start at the top, one line down" then the horizontal line starting going left to right. "One line across"

2. Say "Start at the top - One line down, one line across" as you model a cross shape.

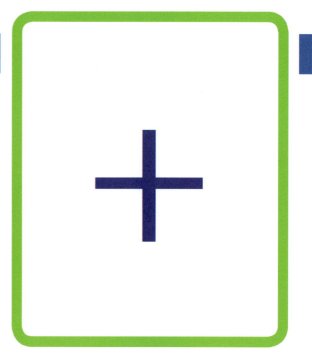

GrowingHandsOnKids.com

Basic Shapes for Beginners

Day 4

WEEK 3

ACTIVITY	AGE LEVEL	PURPOSE
Pipe Cleaner Matching	2-5 Years Old	To promote practice of the cross shape (+) for pre-writing practice

ITEMS NEEDED

- Colored craft pipe cleaners
- Matching cross shape printable
- Task tray

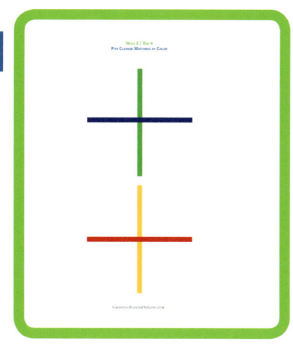

DIRECTIONS

1. Print out the cross shape printable. Have your child match the colored pipe cleaners, using the printable as a guide.

2. Say "Start at the top, One line down, one line across" as you model a cross shape.

CROSS (+) SHAPE

WEEK 3

Basic Shapes for Beginners

DAY 5

CROSS (+) SHAPE

ACTIVITY	AGE LEVEL	PURPOSE
Tracing/Copying Cross Shapes	3-5 Years Old	To promote practice of the cross shape (+) for pre-writing practice

ITEMS NEEDED

- Small golf size pencil or broken crayons
- Cross shapes printable

DIRECTIONS

1. Have your child use the printable to trace and then copy the cross shapes.

2. Say "Start at the top, One line down, one line across" as you model a cross shape.

3. Remember they can lay on their tummies to do this activity for great neck and trunk strengthening!

> Ages 3 and under use a sensory medium such as shaving cream, cornmeal, or finger paint and have them use their fingers to trace the lines instead of using a pencil/crayon

GrowingHandsOnKids.com

Basic Shapes for Beginners

BONUS ACTIVITY

WEEK 3

ACTIVITY	AGE LEVEL	PURPOSE
Chalk Board Copying	3-5 Years Old	To promote practice of the cross shape (+) for pre-writing practice

ITEMS NEEDED

- Chalk board
- Chalk
- Damp wash cloth

Optional: Instead of using a damp wash cloth, you can use different colored pieces of chalk. Have your child trace over each shape with a different color.

DIRECTIONS

1. Have your child lay on their stomach for this activity to get some good trunk strengthening and tummy time.

2. Give them a small chalk board, piece of chalk, and a damp wash cloth.

3. Have them make one line down "Start at the top down" and one line across (left to right) "One line across", using the chalk. Then have them trace over each chalk line with the damp wash cloth, wiping it clean. They can repeat this as many times as they want.

4. If you do not have a chalk board you can use paper and small broken crayons instead. You can still have them use the damp washcloth and wash over the crayon marks.

CROSS (+) SHAPE

Basic Shapes for Beginners

GrowingHandsOnKids.com

Basic Shapes for Beginners

WEEK 4

SUPPLY LIST

- Printables for week 4
- Activity/Task trays
- Small task baskets to organize with
- Laminator and laminator sheets (optional)
- Craft apron/bib
- Scissors
- Small broken crayons
- Small golf size crayons
- Shaving cream
- Food coloring
- Wooden building blocks
- Construction paper
- Marker
- Paper
- Finger paint

SQUARES AND RECTANGLES

WEEK 4

Basic Shapes for Beginners

DAY 1

SQUARES AND RECTANGLES

ACTIVITY	AGE LEVEL	PURPOSE
My House is Made of Shapes Puzzle	2-5 Years Old	Visual motor practice for pre-writing skills

ITEMS NEEDED

- Puzzle Printable
- Scissors
- Crayons
- Laminator and laminator sheets (optional)

DIRECTIONS

1. Print out the puzzle packet.

2. Have your older child (5 and older) trace the sentence at the top of the first page. If your child is younger, you can trace the sentence yourself.

3. Then have your child color all of the individual puzzle pieces. You can choose to laminate these pages now, or wait until the puzzle pieces have been cut out. Cut out each of the pieces with scissors (for younger children you may need to help with this part).

4. They will use the page with the sentence at the top as their "puzzle" board. Simply have them match the shapes to build the house (finished product on the far right picture).

GrowingHandsOnKids.com

Basic Shapes for Beginners

Day 2

WEEK 4

ACTIVITY	AGE LEVEL	PURPOSE
Shaving Cream Squares	2-5 Years Old	Sensory experience for pre-writing skills

ITEMS NEEDED

- Shaving Cream
- Food Coloring
- Task Tray
- Craft Bib/Apron

DIRECTIONS

1. Dispense a small amount of shaving cream onto an activity tray. Place 2-3 drops of food coloring onto the shaving cream and have your child mix it with their hands.

2. Have your child draw vertical and horizontal lines to form squares and rectangles in the shaving cream, using their index/pointer finger. Say: Vertical lines "Straight lines down, start at the top, down."

3. Straight lines across, always start left to right. Say "straight lines across" as your child draws a horizontal line.

SQUARES AND RECTANGLES

GrowingHandsOnKids.com

WEEK 4

Basic Shapes for Beginners

DAY 3

SQUARES AND RECTANGLES

ACTIVITY	AGE LEVEL	PURPOSE
Block Stacking and Building	2-5 Years Old	Visual motor practice for pre-writing skills

ITEMS NEEDED

- Wooden building blocks

DIRECTIONS

Have your child practice stacking building blocks in the following designs, modeling each design for them:

- Tower
- Train
- Bridge
- Pyramid

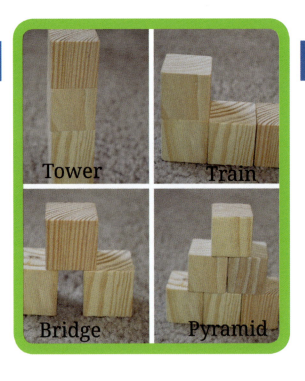

GrowingHandsOnKids.com

BASIC SHAPES FOR BEGINNERS

DAY 4

WEEK 4

ACTIVITY	AGES APPROPRIATE	PURPOSE
Paper Strip Cutting Activity	3-5 Years Old	Visual motor practice for pre-writing skills

ITEMS NEEDED

- Construction paper
- Scissors
- Marker

If your child is over 3 years old, have then cut along each line, cutting the paper into 4 strips.

DIRECTIONS

1. Have your child pick a sheet of construction paper.

2. Draw 4 vertical lines from the top to the bottom of the page.

3. Last, have your child pick up one strip and practice cutting the strip into square shapes. You can draw lines across each strip for them to cut on, however I would suggest letting them try without the cutting lines first. Judging where to cut to make the paper strip into a square is a great visual motor skill.

4. You can use the small pieces that they cut to make a collage or design with glue on another piece of construction paper if you like.

SQUARES AND RECTANGLES

GROWINGHANDSONKIDS.COM

WEEK 4

Basic Shapes for Beginners

DAY 5

SQUARES AND RECTANGLES

ACTIVITY	AGE LEVEL	PURPOSE
Build Your House	2-5 Years Old	Visual motor practice for pre-writing skills

ITEMS NEEDED

- Wooden craft sticks
- Task Tray

DIRECTIONS

Have your child use craft sticks of various sizes to design what they think their house looks like.

GrowingHandsOnKids.com

Basic Shapes for Beginners

BONUS ACTIVITY

WEEK 4

SQUARES AND RECTANGLES

ACTIVITY	AGE LEVEL	PURPOSE
Tracing & Copying Square Shapes	3-5 Years Old	Visual motor practice for pre-writing skills

ITEMS NEEDED

- Square & Rectangle Printable
- Small pencil (golf size) or marker
- Small or broken crayons

Ages 3 and under use a sensory medium such as shaving cream, cornmeal, or finger paint and have them use their fingers to trace the lines instead of using a pencil/crayon

DIRECTIONS

1. Print out the tracing printable

2. Have your child trace each shape and then color them.

GrowingHandsOnKids.com

41

Basic Shapes for Beginners

GrowingHandsOnKids.com

BASIC SHAPES FOR BEGINNERS

WEEK 5

X SHAPE AND DIAGONAL LINES

SUPPLY LIST

- Printables for week 5
- Activity/Task trays
- Small task baskets to organize with
- Homemade or store bought finger paint (2-3 colors)
- Paint Brushes (Optional)
- Painting bib
- Colored craft pipe cleaners
- Wikki stix
- Homemade or store bought play dough
- Cotton balls
- Paint cups
- Long wooden craft dowel rods
- Wooden skinny sticks
- Golf size/small pencil
- Broken/Small crayons
- Finger paint

GrowingHandsOnKids.com

43

Basic Shapes for Beginners

WEEK 5

DAY 1

X SHAPE AND DIAGONAL LINES

ACTIVITY	AGE LEVEL	PURPOSE
Finger Paint Brushing	3-5 Years Old	Sensory Experience for Pre-writing Skills

ITEMS NEEDED

- Homemade or store bought finger paint (2-3 colors)
- Paint Brushes (Optional)
- Diagonal & X Line Printable
- Painting bib

DIRECTIONS

1. Print out the diagonal and "X" line printable. You can place it on top of a large piece of paper to help keep the paint off your table, or a large trash bag. In the summer time or warm weather months, you can also do this outside!

2. Provide your child with the finger paint, painting brush (optional) or have them use their index fingers.

3. Have them trace each line, starting at the top. For "X" Shapes always start with the line from the top left first.

GrowingHandsOnKids.com

Basic Shapes for Beginners

Day 2

WEEK 5

ACTIVITY	AGE LEVEL	PURPOSE
Matching Diagonal & X Shape Lines	2-5 Years Old	Sensory & Visual Motor Experience for Pre-writing Skills

ITEMS NEEDED

- X and diagonal line printable
- Colored pipe cleaners or Wikki stix
- Task Tray

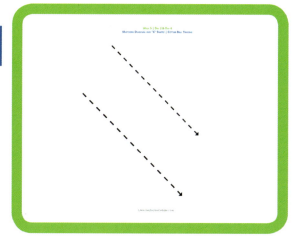

DIRECTIONS

1. Print out the X and diagonal lines matching printable and place it on a task tray.

2. Have a container of colored pipe cleaners or Wikki stix next to the task tray and have your child place the piper cleaners or Wikki stix on top of each shape.

X SHAPE AND DIAGONAL LINES

GrowingHandsOnKids.com

45

WEEK 5

Basic Shapes for Beginners

DAY 3

X SHAPE AND DIAGONAL LINES

ACTIVITY	AGE LEVEL	PURPOSE
Play Dough Lines	2-5 Years Old	Sensory Experience for Pre-writing Skills

ITEMS NEEDED

- Homemade or store bought play dough
- Task Tray

DIRECTIONS

1. Have your child make "X" shapes out of play dough. First by rolling out straight lines using their hands and then placing each line into a "X" shape on their task tray.

2. You can easily add in other shapes such as straight/horizontal lines, circle shapes, cross shapes and squares/rectangles to reinforce previous shapes and lines.

GrowingHandsOnKids.com

Basic Shapes for Beginners

DAY 4

WEEK 5

X SHAPE AND DIAGONAL LINES

ACTIVITY	AGE LEVEL	PURPOSE
Cotton Ball Tracing	2-5 Years Old	Sensory & Visual Motor Experience for Pre-writing Skills

ITEMS NEEDED

- Cotton Balls
- Finger Paint
- Paint cups
- "X" and diagonal lines printable
- Task Tray
- Painting Bib

Example: For Left Diagonal line - "Start at the top left, line sideways" For Right Diagonal line - "Start at the top right, line sideways" "X" - X marks the spot!

DIRECTIONS

1. Set up your task tray with a large trash bag or craft paper underneath to catch any drips. Set up the finger paint in individual painting cups and also have cotton balls in a mini container next to the paint. Have your child wear a painting bib as well.

2. Have them use a pincer grasp on the cotton balls, dip them into the finger paint, and use them to trace over the "X" shape and diagonal lines. Be sure to use the same language when describing the lines to your child.

GrowingHandsOnKids.com

47

WEEK 5

Basic Shapes for Beginners

DAY 5

X SHAPE AND DIAGONAL LINES

ACTIVITY	AGE LEVEL	PURPOSE
DIY Tic Tac Toe Board	3-5 Years Old	Sensory & Visual Motor Experience for Pre-writing Skills

ITEMS NEEDED

- Long wooden craft dowel rods
- Wooden skinny sticks
- Colored craft pipe cleaners
- Task boxes
- Task Tray

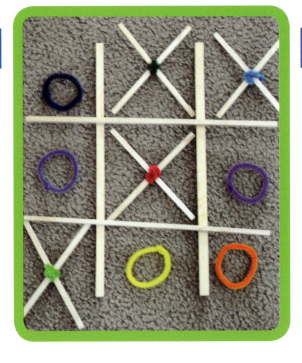

DIRECTIONS

1. The first thing you are going to do is have your child make the tic tac toe board out of the long wooden craft dowel rods.

2. Have your child take two wooden sticks and make an "X" shape.

3. Wrap the two sticks together where they meet for the "X" with a pipe cleaner to hold them together.

4. For the circle shape, take a pipe cleaner and form into a circle, twisting the ends together and laying them flat against the sides

5. Now it's time to play a game of tic tac toe!

GrowingHandsOnKids.com

Basic Shapes for Beginners

BONUS ACTIVITY

WEEK 5

ACTIVITY	AGE LEVEL	PURPOSE
Tracing & Copying Diagonal Lines & "X" Shape	3-5 Years Old	Visual Motor and Fine Motor skills practice for pre-writing skills

ITEMS NEEDED

- Diagonal line & "X" Shape printable
- Golf size/small pencil
- Broken/Small crayons

> Ages 3 and under use a sensory medium such as shaving cream, cornmeal, or finger paint and have them use their fingers to trace the lines instead of using a pencil/crayon.

DIRECTIONS

1. Print out the diagonal and "X" shape printable.

2. Have your child practice tracing (Age 3-4) or copying (age 4-5) the shapes following your verbal direction:

   For Left Diagonal line say - "Start at the top left, line sideways"

   For Right Diagonal line say - "Start at the top right, line sideways"

   "X" say - X marks the spot!

X SHAPE AND DIAGONAL LINES

GrowingHandsOnKids.com

Basic Shapes for Beginners

GrowingHandsOnKids.com

Basic Shapes for Beginners

WEEK 6

TRIANGLES AND DIAMONDS

SUPPLY LIST

- Printables for week 6
- Activity/Task trays
- Small task baskets to organize with
- Small or broken crayons
- Scissors
- Glue
- Hole punch
- Craft pipe cleaners
- Homemade or store bought play dough
- Diamond or triangle cookie cutters
- Play dough cutting tools
- Sensory medium (such as couscous, rice, lentils, small noodles etc.)
- Craft foam sheets or kitchen sponges
- Scissors
- Marker
- Paper
- Finger paint
- Painting Bib
- Q-Tips
- Paper or small chalk board (optional)
- Marker or chalk
- Bowl of water
- Colored Glitter Glue (Optional)
- Paper

WEEK 6

Basic Shapes for Beginners

DAY 1

TRIANGLES AND DIAMONDS

ACTIVITY	AGE LEVEL	PURPOSE
Triangle & Diamond Coloring Sheet	2-5 Years Old	Fine motor skill and visual motor skill practice for pre-writing lines

ITEMS NEEDED

- Triangle and diamond coloring sheet
- Small or broken crayons

DIRECTIONS

1. Print out the triangle and diamond coloring sheet.

2. Have your child follow the directions for coloring each shape.

3. Remember to have your child practice proper grasp on their crayons when coloring and to stay inside the lines as best they can.

> Ages 3 and under use a sensory medium such as colored shaving cream or finger paint and have them use their fingers to color instead of using crayons/pencils.

GrowingHandsOnKids.com

Basic Shapes for Beginners

Day 2

WEEK 6

ACTIVITY	AGE LEVEL	PURPOSE
Paper Crown Craft	2-5 Years Old	Fine motor skill and visual motor skill practice for pre-writing lines

ITEMS NEEDED

- Crown template
- Diamond shape cutout printable
- Scissors
- Glue
- Hole punch
- Craft Pipe Cleaners
- Small or broken crayons

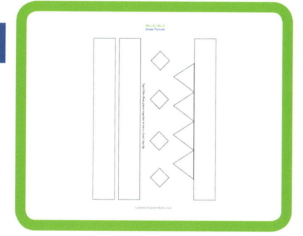

DIRECTIONS

1. Print out the crown and diamond shape printables and have your child color each one using the small or broken crayons. For ages 3+ have them cut out the diamonds and crown shape. For younger ages, you will probably need to cut out the shapes yourself.

2. Have your child decorate their crown using the diamond shapes by gluing them onto the crown template.

3. Use a hole punch to cut out one hole on either side of the crown template. Wrap a pipe cleaner through each hole and then connect each pipe cleaner together to fit around your child's head.

TRIANGLES AND DIAMONDS

GrowingHandsOnKids.com

53

WEEK 6

TRIANGLES AND DIAMONDS

Basic Shapes for Beginners

DAY 3

ACTIVITY	AGE LEVEL	PURPOSE
Play dough cut outs	2-5 Years Old	Fine motor skill and visual motor skill practice for pre-writing lines

ITEMS NEEDED

- Homemade or store bought play dough
- Diamond or triangle cookie cutters (You can use play dough cutting tools instead if you don't have the shape cookie cutters)
- Task tray

DIRECTIONS

1. Have your child flatten out the play dough on their task tray.

2. Using the cookie cutters or the play dough cutting tools, have them cut out diamond and triangle shapes out of the play dough.

Optional: You can have them organize each shape they cut out into other smaller task trays (Ex. putting all the diamond shapes into one tray and all the triangle shapes in another tray)

Basic Shapes for Beginners

Day 4

WEEK 6

ACTIVITY	AGE LEVEL	PURPOSE
Sensory Tracing	2-5 Years Old	Fine motor skill and visual motor skill practice for pre-writing lines

ITEMS NEEDED

- Diamond and triangle printable
- Sensory medium (such as couscous, cornmeal, rice, lentils, small noodles etc.)
- Task Tray

DIRECTIONS

1. Print out the diamond and triangle printable and place it on a task tray.

2. Cover the printable with a thin layer of your sensory medium (couscous is pictured below).

3. Have your child trace each shape through the sensory medium. You may need to mark a starting point for younger children (3 and under).

TRIANGLES AND DIAMONDS

GrowingHandsOnKids.com

55

WEEK 6

Basic Shapes for Beginners

DAY 5

TRIANGLES AND DIAMONDS

ACTIVITY	AGE LEVEL	PURPOSE
Foam Shape Stamping	2-5 Years Old	Fine motor skill and visual motor skill practice for pre-writing lines

ITEMS NEEDED

- Craft foam sheets or kitchen sponges
- Scissors
- Marker
- Paper
- Finger paint - store bought works best
- Painting Bib

DIRECTIONS

1. Draw triangle and diamond shapes on the foam sheets/kitchen sponge, large enough for your child to cut them out. Have your child (Ages 4+) cut out each shape and set them aside.

2. Have a task tray set up with the paper and finger paint. Use the shapes as stamps in the finger paint. Your child can use them to make a picture of their choosing.

GrowingHandsOnKids.com

Basic Shapes for Beginners

BONUS ACTIVITY

WEEK 6

ACTIVITY	AGE LEVEL	PURPOSE
Q-Tip Tracing	2-5 Years Old	Fine motor skill and visual motor skill practice for pre-writing lines

ITEMS NEEDED

- Q-Tips
- Paper or small chalk board (optional)
- Marker or chalk
- Bowl of water
- Colored glitter glue (Optional)
- Paper

Bonus: Have your child do this activity on their tummy to get in some good trunk and neck strengthening.

DIRECTIONS

For Chalk Board: Draw a triangle shape, then diamond shape with chalk and have your child trace over it using the wet Q-Tip to trace over the lines.

For Paper: Draw triangle and diamond shapes (various sizes) on a piece of paper. Place the paper on a task tray and have your child trace over the shapes using the Q-tip dipped into the glitter glue. Let it dry before hanging.

TRIANGLES AND DIAMONDS

GrowingHandsOnKids.com

57

RESOURCES

For more resources to products that will help you with these 6 weeks of activities visit the page below.

growinghandsonkids.com/basic-shapes-resources

HOW TO DOWNLOAD THE PRINTABLES

Visit:
growinghandsonkids.com/basic-shapes-printables

Download the printables and save to your computer. Print them to go with corresponding activities in this book.

You will need the password below to open the PDF:

BSB77!

These printables are for your access only. Please do not share this page or password with others.

If you have problems accessing the printables, e-mail:

heather@growinghandsonkids.com

with the subject line **Basic Shapes Printables**.

ABOUT THE AUTHOR

Heather Greutman is a Certified Occupational Therapy Assistant turned therapy/homeschool mom blogger. She writes at *Growing Hands-On Kids* where her goal is to encourage independence, one activity at a time. She loves spending time with her husband and two children, creating fun and engaging activities, photography, coffee, and writing.

facebook.com/growinghandsonkids

twitter.com/growhandsonkids

pinterest.com/growhandsonkids

instagram.com/growinghandsonkids

PRINTABLES

Week 1 | Day 1
Matching Vertical and Horizontal Lines

GrowingHandsOnKids.com

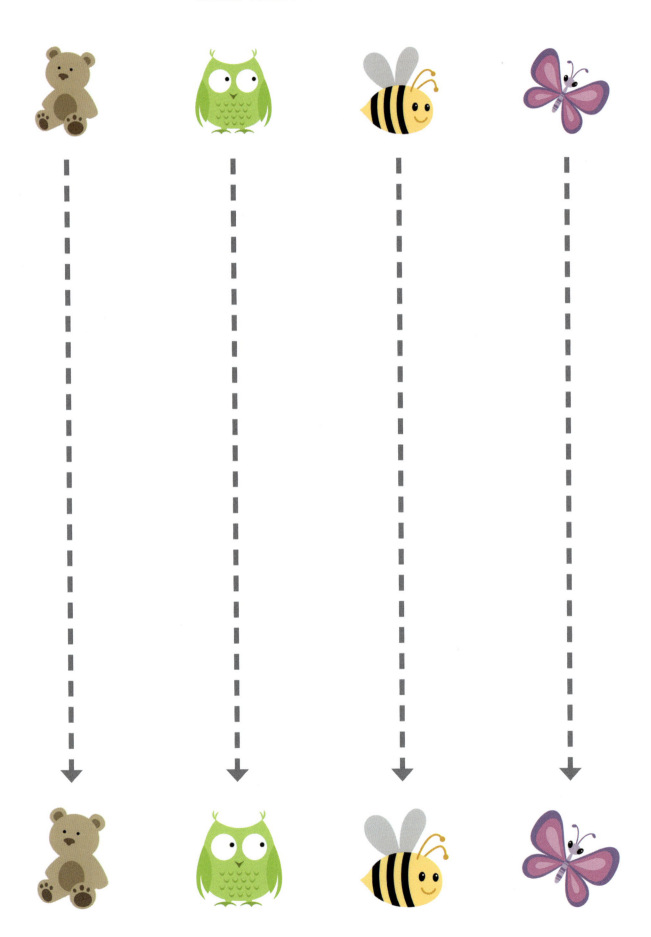

Week 1 | Day 3
Tracing Vertical and Horizontal Lines

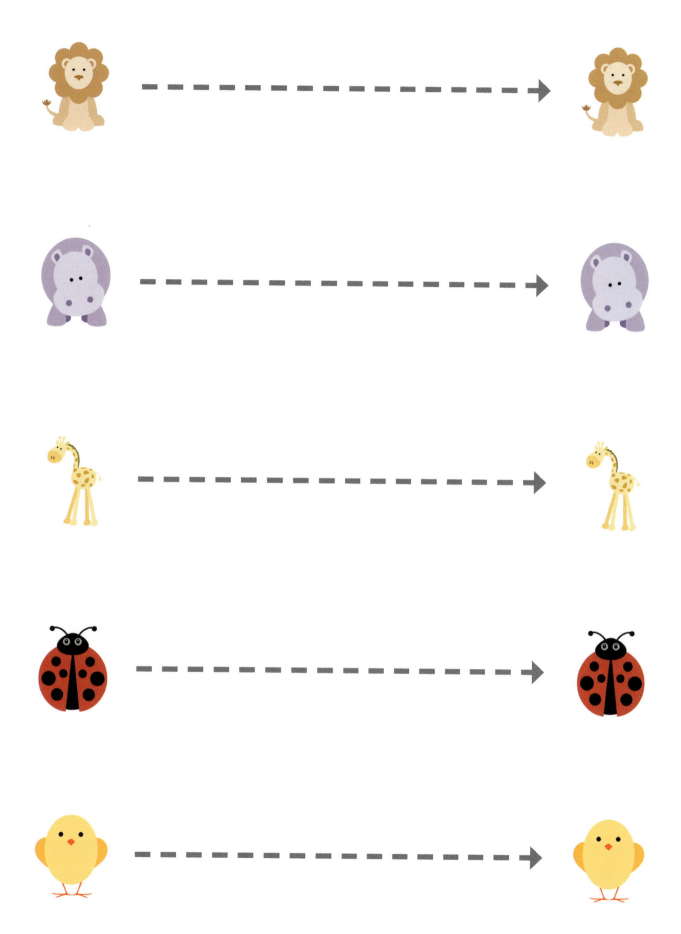

GrowingHandsOnKids.com

Week 1 | Day 5
Coloring Vertical and Horizontal Lines

Color the big lines RED. Color the small lines BLUE

Week 2 | Day 4
Circle Coloring Sheet

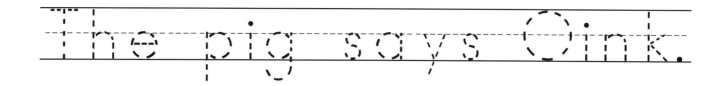

The pig says Oink.

GROWINGHANDSONKIDS.COM

Week 2 | Day 5
Trace or Copy Circle Shapes

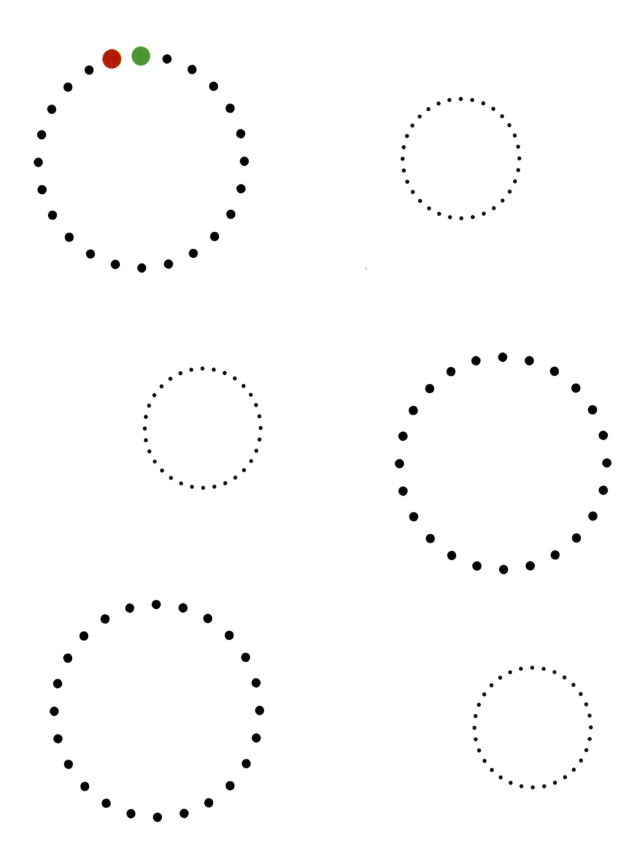

GROWINGHANDSONKIDS.COM

Week 3 | Day 1
Crossing Midline Parade

GrowingHandsOnKids.com

Week 3 | Day 1
Crossing Midline Parade

GrowingHandsOnKids.com

Week 3 | Day 2
Figure 8 Motor Walk

Printable should be placed horizontally on the writing surface.

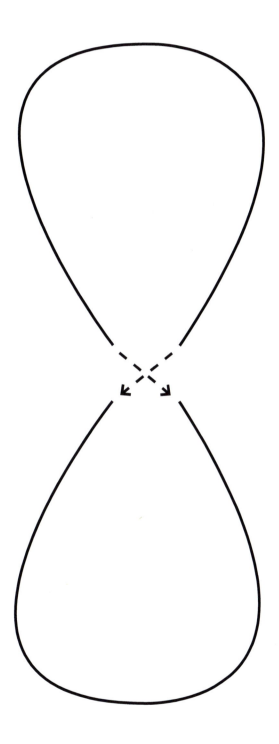

GROWINGHANDSONKIDS.COM

Week 3 | Day 4
Pipe Cleaner Matching by Color

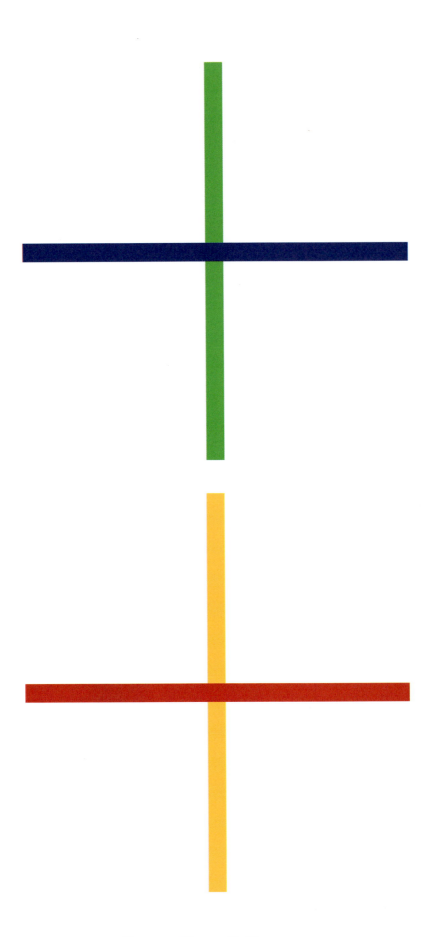

GrowingHandsOnKids.com

Week 3 | Day 4
Pipe Cleaner Matching by Color

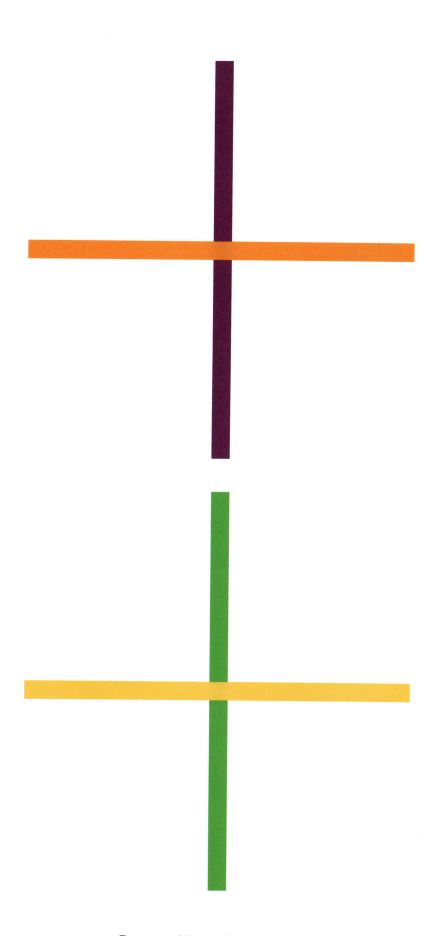

Week 3 | Day 4
Pipe Cleaner Matching by Color

GrowingHandsOnKids.com

Week 3 | Day 5
Tracing and Copying Cross Shapes

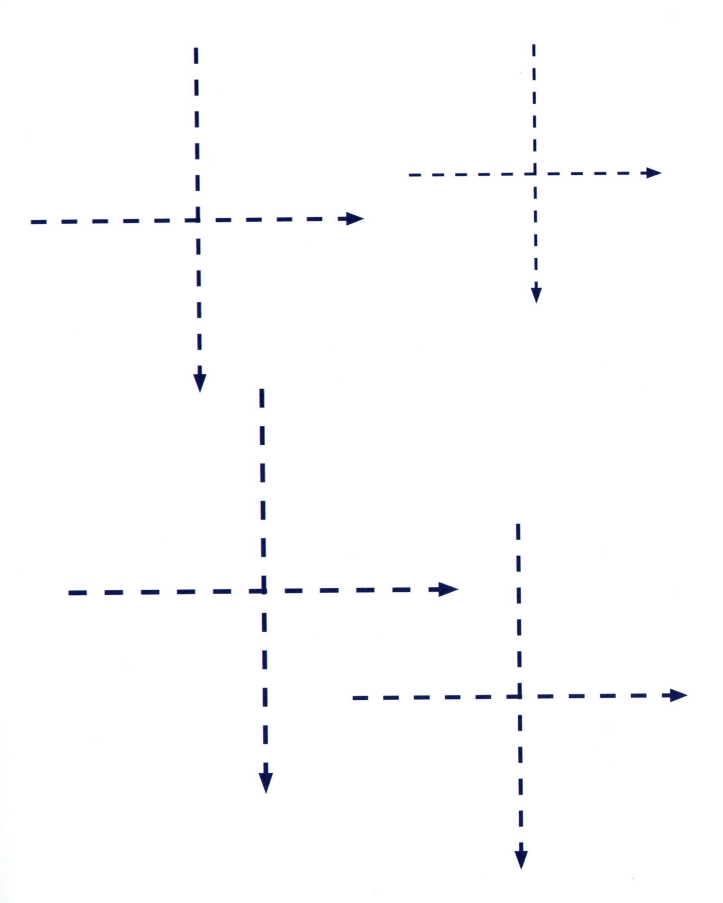

GrowingHandsOnKids.com

Week 4 | Day 1
My House is Made of Shapes Puzzle

My house is made of squares, triangles, and rectangles.

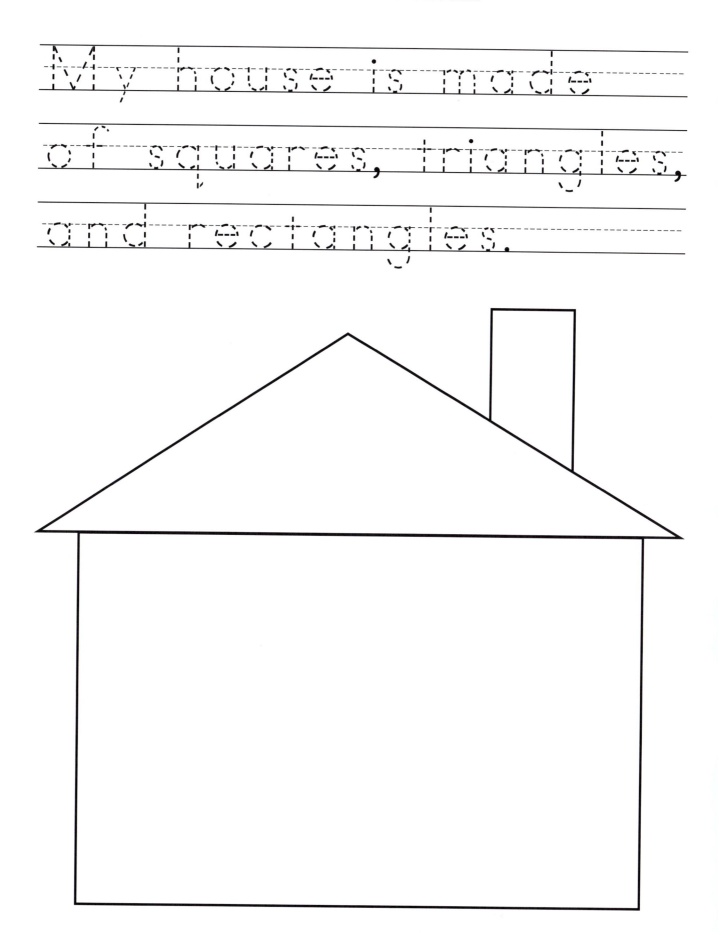

This page intentionally left blank.

Week 4 | Day 1
My House is Made of Shapes Puzzle

Have your child color all the shapes you see below. In the large rectangle piece at the bottom, have your child color the entire thing the same color. The windows and door in this piece are only guides for where to put the puzzle pieces. Cut out these shapes with scissors. If you are working with a smaller child (under 3, possibly 4 depending on their scissor skills) you may want to cut the shapes out yourself and just have them place the pieces on the house above.

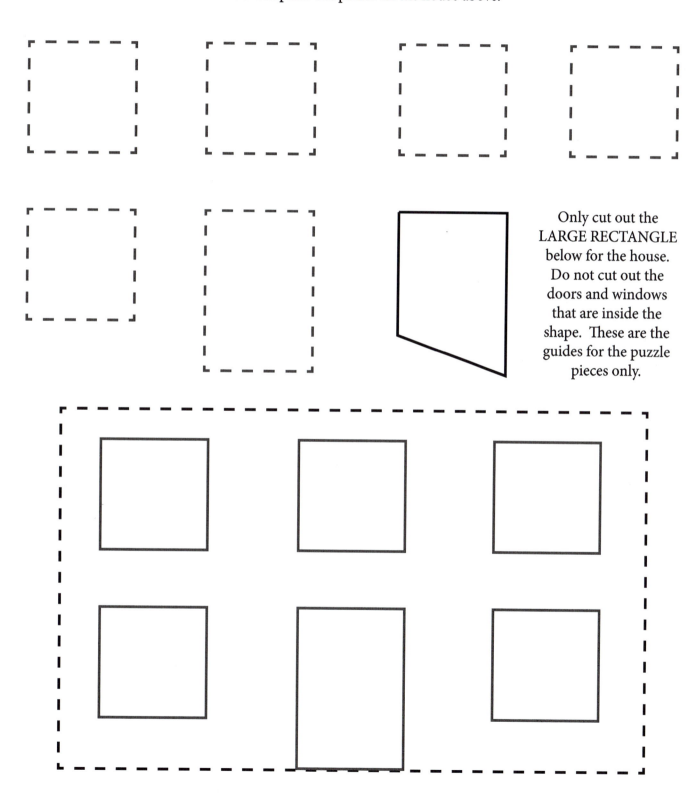

Only cut out the LARGE RECTANGLE below for the house. Do not cut out the doors and windows that are inside the shape. These are the guides for the puzzle pieces only.

GrowingHandsOnKids.com

This page intentionally left blank.

GrowingHandsOnKids.com

Week 4 | Day 1
My House is Made of Shapes Puzzle

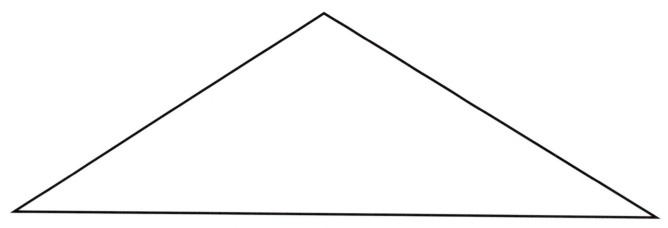

Optional: Have your child draw horizontal and vertical lines in the windows to practice drawing straight lines and cross shapes.

GROWINGHANDSONKIDS.COM

This page intentionally left blank.

GrowingHandsOnKids.com

Week 4 | Bonus Activity
Tracing and Copying Square Shapes

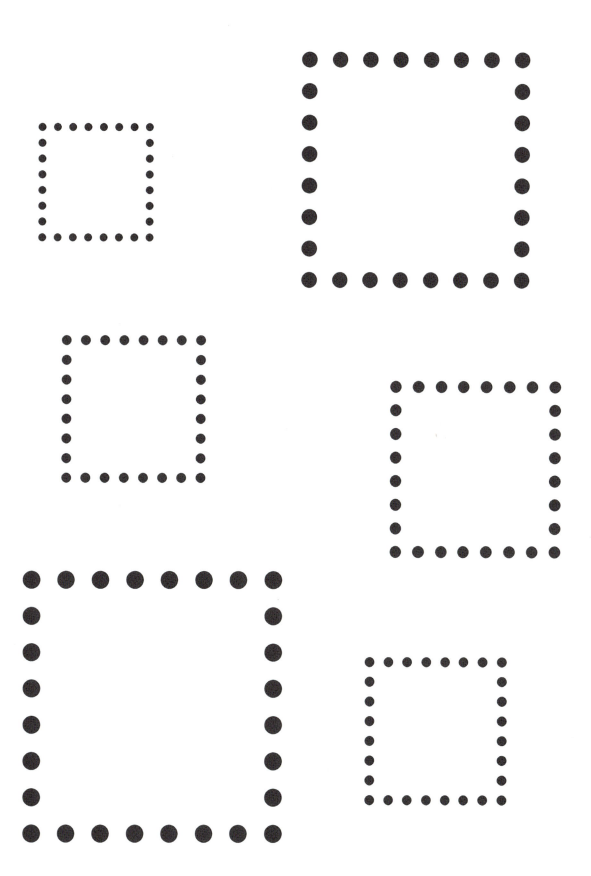

GrowingHandsOnKids.com

Week 5 | Day 1, Day 4, and Bonus Activity

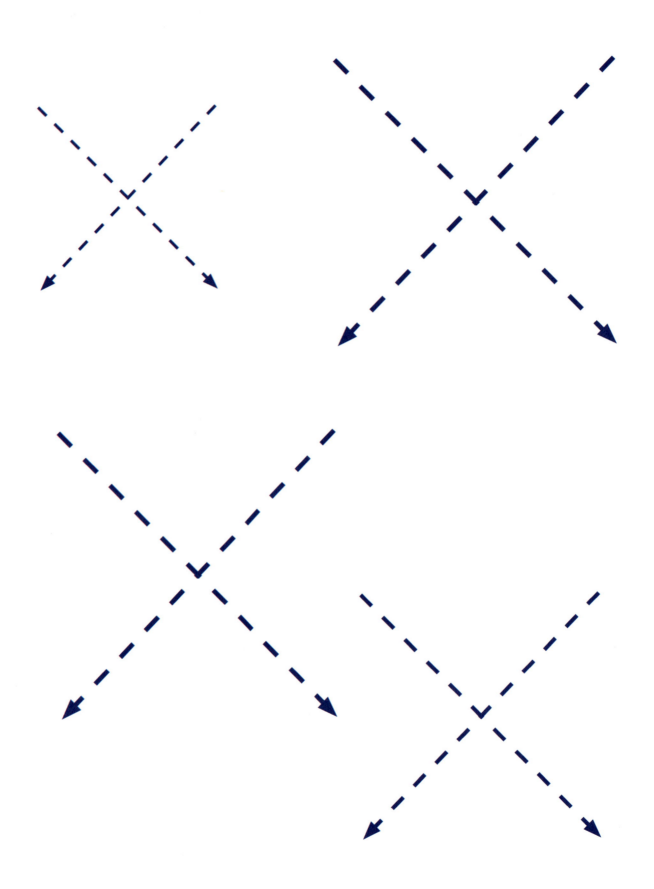

GrowingHandsOnKids.com

Week 5 | Day 1, Day 4, and Bonus Activity

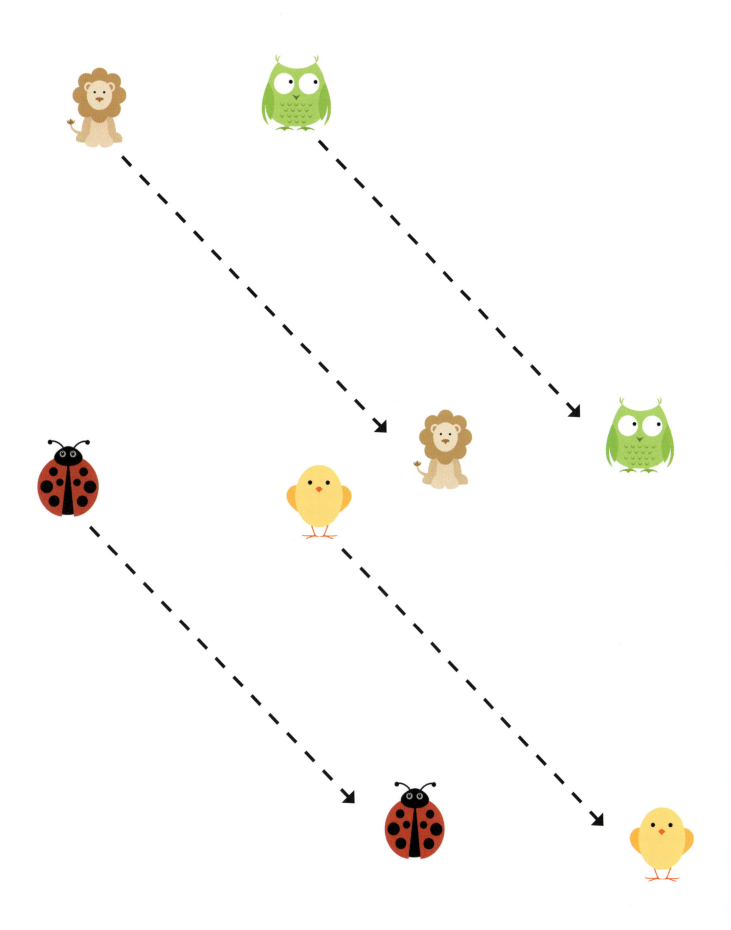

GrowingHandsOnKids.com

Week 5 | Day 1, Day 4, and Bonus Activity

GrowingHandsOnKids.com

Week 5 | Day 2 & Day 4
Matching Diagonal and "X" Shapes | Cotton Ball Tracing

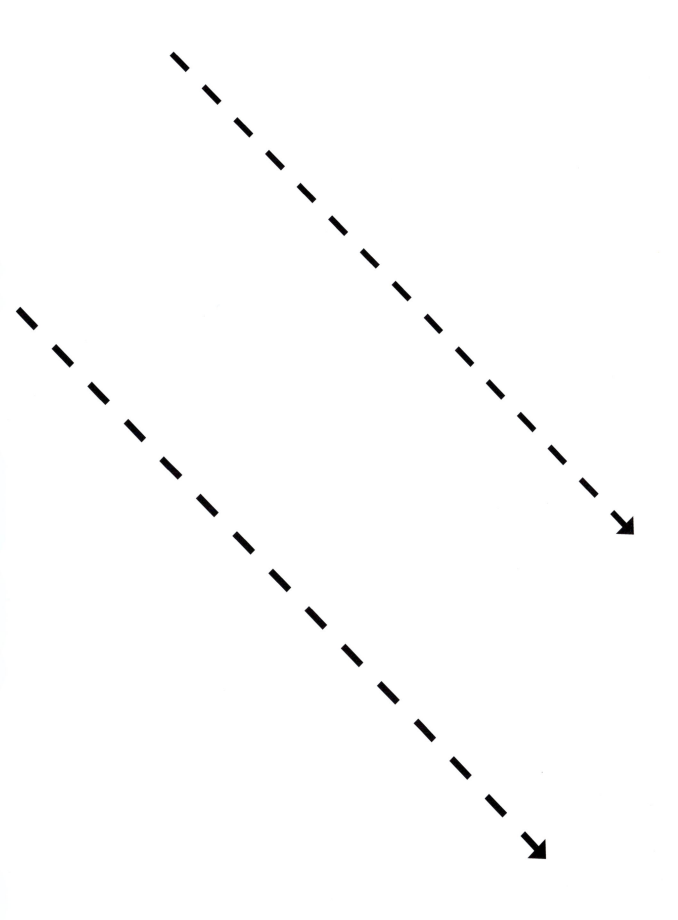

GrowingHandsOnKids.com

Week 5 | Day 2 & Day 4
Matching Diagonal and "X" Shapes | Cotton Ball Tracing

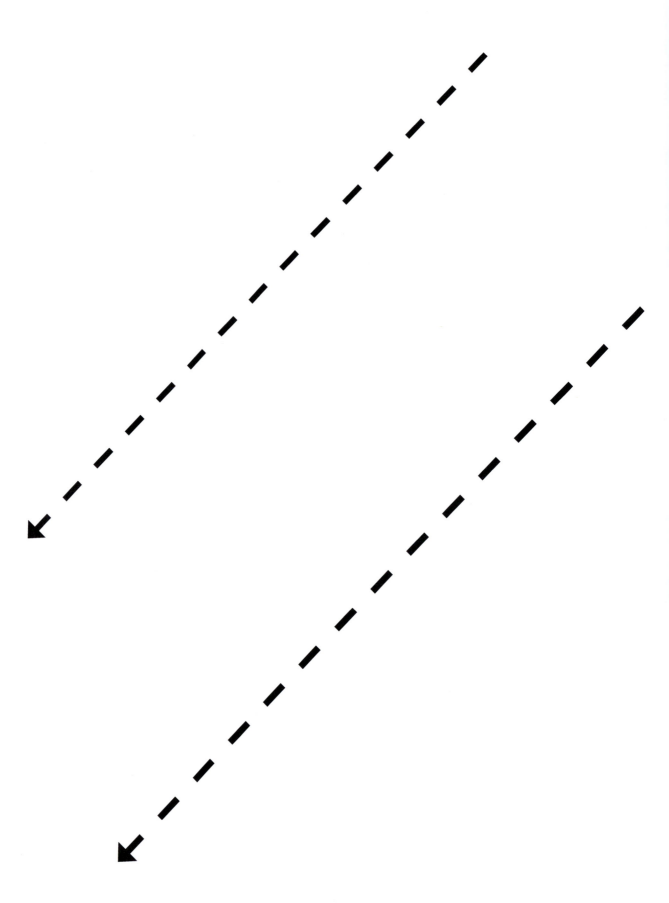

GrowingHandsOnKids.com

Week 5 | Day 2 & Day 4
Matching Diagonal and "X" Shapes | Cotton Ball Tracing

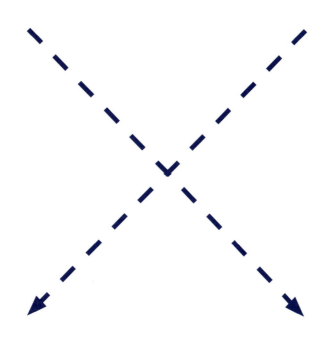

GrowingHandsOnKids.com

Week 6 | Day 1
Triangle and Diamond Coloring Sheet

Color the big triangles RED

Color the small triangles BLUE

Color the little diamonds YELLOW

Color the big diamonds GREEN

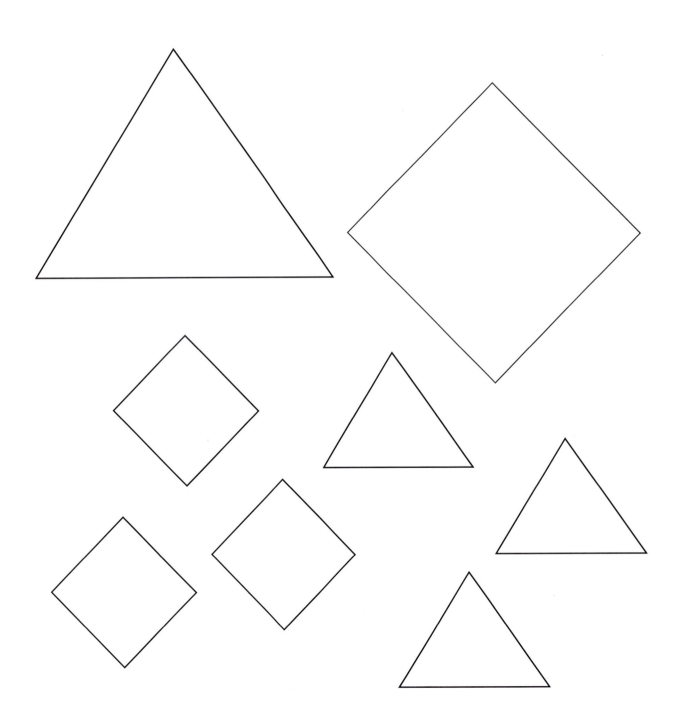

GrowingHandsOnKids.com

Week 6 | Day 2
Crown Template

GROWINGHANDSONKIDS.COM

This page intentionally left blank.

Week 6 | Day 4
Diamond and Triangle Sensory Shape Tracing

Diamond and Triangle Shape Model

Cover the paper with rice, couscous, quinoa, or sand and have your child trace each shape, also moving the sensory item to the edge of each shape.

Which one is smaller and which one is bigger?

Dump off the sensory item and then have them trace each shape with a crayon, marker, or pencil, using an age appropriate pencil grasp.

Again have them point out which one is smaller and which one is bigger.

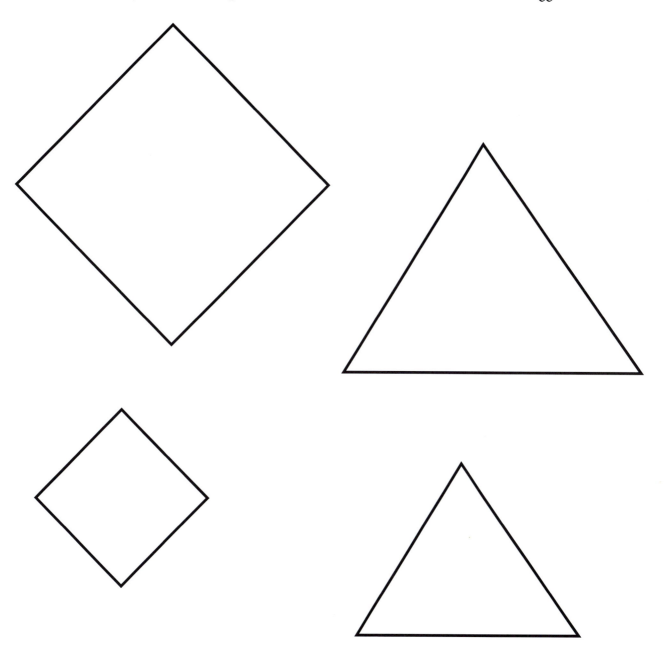

GrowingHandsOnKids.com

BONUS SHAPE - STAR COLOR PAGE

Color the big stars RED

Color the little stars BLUE

GROWINGHANDSONKIDS.COM

Bonus Shape - Tracing Star Shapes with Shaving Cream

GROWINGHANDSONKIDS.COM

THIS PAGE INTENTIONALLY LEFT BLANK.

BONUS SHAPE - "I HEART YOU!" CARD

THIS PAGE INTENTIONALLY LEFT BLANK.

Printed in Great Britain
by Amazon